PRE-APPRENTICESHIP
MATHS & LITERACY FOR
PLASTERING & RENDERING

Graduated exercises and practice exam

Andrew Spencer

A+ National Pre-apprenticeship Maths & Literacy for Plastering & Rendering
1st Edition
Andrew Spencer

Publishing editors: Sarah Broomhall and Jennifer Down
Project editor: Aynslie Harper
Text designer: Miranda Costa
Cover designer: Aisling Gallagher
Cover image: Shutterstock.com/bouybin
Permissions researcher: Kait Jordan
Production controller: Emily Moore
Typeset by: Q2A Media
Reprint: Katie McCappin

Any URLs contained in this publication were checked for currency during the production process. Note, however, that the publisher cannot vouch for the ongoing currency of URLs.

For product information and technology assistance,
in Australia call **1300 790 853**;
in New Zealand call **0800 449 725**

For permission to use material from this text or product, please email
aust.permissions@cengage.com

ISBN 978 0 17 047452 8

Cengage Learning Australia
Level 7, 80 Dorcas Street
South Melbourne, Victoria Australia 3205

Cengage Learning New Zealand
Unit 4B Rosedale Office Park
331 Rosedale Road, Albany, North Shore 0632, NZ

For learning solutions, visit **cengage.com.au**

Printed in Australia by Ligare Pty Limited.
1 2 3 4 5 6 7 26 25 24 23 22

A+ National
PRE-APPRENTICESHIP
Maths & Literacy for Plastering and Rendering

Contents

Introduction

It has always been important to understand, from a teacher's perspective, the nature of the mathematical skills students need for their future, rather than teaching them 'textbook mathematics'. This has been a guiding principle behind the development of the content in this workbook. To teach maths that is *relevant* to students seeking apprenticeships is the best that we can do, to give students an education in the field that they would like to work in.

The content in this resource is aimed at the level that is needed for students to have the best possibility of improving their maths and literacy skills specifically for trades. Students can use this workbook to prepare for an apprenticeship entry assessment, or even to assist with basic numeracy and literacy at the VET/TAFE level. Coupled with the activities on the NelsonNet website, https://www.nelsonnet.com.au/free-resources, these resources have the potential to improve the students' understanding of basic mathematical concepts that can be applied to trades. These resources have been trialled, and they work.

Commonly used trade terms are introduced so that students have a basic understanding of terminology that they will encounter in the workplace environment. Students who can complete this workbook and reach an 80 per cent or higher outcome in all topics will have achieved the goal of this resource. These students will go on to complete work experience, do a VET accredited course, or will be able to gain entry into VET/TAFE or an apprenticeship in the trade of their choice.

The content in this workbook is the first step to bridging the gap between what has been learnt in previous years, and what needs to be remembered and re-learnt for use in trades. Students will significantly benefit from the consolidation of the basic maths and literacy concepts.

Every school has students who want to work with their hands, and not all students want to go to university. The best students want to learn what they don't already know, and if students want to learn, then this book has the potential to give them a good start in life.

This resource has been specifically tailored to prepare students for sitting apprenticeship or VET/TAFE admission tests, and for giving students the basic skills they will need for a career in trade. In many ways, it is a win–win situation, with students enjoying and studying relevant maths for work, and for Trades and Registered Training Officers (RTOs) receiving students who have improved basic maths and literacy skills.

All that is needed from students is patience, hard work, a positive attitude, a belief in themselves that they can do it and a desire to achieve.

About the author

Andrew Spencer graduated from SACAE Underdale in 1988 with a Bachelor of Education. In 1989, he went on to attend West Virginia University, where he completed a Master of Science (specialising in teacher education), while lecturing part time.

In 1993, Andrew moved to NSW and began teaching at Sydney Boys' High, where he taught in a range of subject areas including Mathematics, English, Science, Classics, Physical Education and Technical Studies. His sense of practical mathematics continued to develop with the range of subject areas he taught.

Andrew moved back to South Australia in 1997 with a diverse knowledge base and an understanding of the importance of using mathematics in different practical subject areas. He began teaching with the De La Salle Brothers in 1997 in South Australia, where he continues to work and teach today. Andrew has worked in collaboration with the SACE Board to help develop resources for Mathematics with a practical focus.

In 2011, Andrew was awarded the John Gaffney Mathematics Education Trust Award for valuable contributions to the teaching of Mathematics in South Australia. He received a Recognition of Excellence for outstanding contributions to the teaching profession by CEASA in 2011 and 2012 and, in 2014, he was one of 12 teachers from across Australia to work in collaboration with the Chief Scientist of Australia to develop a better understanding of the role of mathematics in industry. As part of this role, he undertook research in this area, spent time working with the industry, and then fed the results back to the Chief Scientist.

Andrew continues to develop the pre-apprenticeship and vocational titles, based on mathematics and literacy, to assist and support the learning of students who want to follow a vocational career path. The titles have also been adapted in the UK and Asia, as the importance of this type of functional maths continues to grow. All schools have students who will follow a vocational pathway and it continues to be a strong focus of Andrew's to support the learning needs of these students.

Author acknowledgements

For Paula, Zach, Katelyn, Mum and Dad.

To the De La Salle Brothers for their selfless work with all students.

To Dr Pauline Carter for her unwavering support of all Mathematics teachers.

To all students who value learning, who are willing to work hard and who have character … and are characters!

LITERACY

Unit 1: Spelling

Short-answer questions

Specific instructions to students

- This is an exercise to help you to identify and correct spelling errors.
- Read the activity below and then answer accordingly.

Read the following passage, and identify and correct the spelling errors.

Brent wanted to rendar a brick wall but had no idea where to begin, so he asked his quallified mate, Matt. 'What do I need to do first?' Brent asked. 'Well,' Matt replied, 'first, you will need to use a stele brush to remoove any loose material that could affect good adhesian. Second, try to remove any old, hard mortar in the joints of the walls. Third, make sure you cover all floors, paths or driveways with plastik sheets, to protect them from any spilt render. You'll also need to mask any other exposed surfaces that you want kept clean.' Equipped with this advice, Brent began the work.

'Oh, and I nearly forgot', sparked up Matt. 'You'll need to fix the corner beeding to the outar corners of the surface to be rendered. You will need to use an adheysive that has been approved to ensure that it is straight and plummb. This will help to delivar an acurate rendered finish.' 'Ok', replied Brent, who was eager to continue working.

'Oh, and another thing, Brent. Don't forget to apply a small ammount of render to the inside of the beading and make sure that you press it well into the corner. Any exces render needs to be cleaned off too.' 'Thanks, Matt. I think I'm all set now. Cheers!' replied Brent.

Brent pushed a wheelbarow to a tap so that he could pour some water into it. 'Gee, I'm not sure how much water I'll need', mummbled Brent. 'What did it say on the bag, Brent?' Matt called out. 'Hang on, I'll read it', replied Brent.

'I think I need to por four litres of water into the wheelbarrow and then pour one bag of render into the water slowly.' 'Is that what it says on the bag?' yelled Matt. 'Yeah!' replied Brent. 'Nice one, Brent! Always read the instructions before you start, mate!' Brent then read the remaynder of the instructions and began to pour the water into the wheelbarrow, but he only poured four litres of clean water to begin with.

Incorrect words:

_____

_____

Correct words:

_____

_____

Unit 2: Alphabetising

Short-answer questions

Specific instructions to students

- In this unit, you will be able to practise your alphabetising skills.
- Read the activity below and then answer accordingly.

Put the following words into alphabetical order.

Float	Levelling
Hawk	OHS
Render	Coats
Drill	Blockwork
Mixer	Trestle
Communication	Planks
Measure	Dash coat
Prepare	Water
Plaster	Metal trowel
Scaffold	Cornices

Answer:

_____

_____

_____

_____

_____

_____

_____

_____

_____

_____

_____

_____

_____

_____

_____

_____

_____

_____

_____

_____

Unit 3: Comprehension

Short-answer questions

Specific instructions to students

- This is an exercise to help you understand what you read.
- Read the following activity and then answer the questions that follow.

Read the following passage and answer the questions in full sentences.

It is preferable to fix plasterboard to an existing ceiling, and it is important to determine where the joists are. If the plasterboard is being fixed to a second-floor ceiling, the joist gaps in the loft can be measured to help find the joists. The joist gaps can be marked on the wall with chalk prior to beginning. One other option is to remove the existing ceiling to expose the joists. Plasterboard needs to be well supported wherever it is being fixed. In some cases, there might not be any wood between where the joists meet the wall. If this happens, some noggings need to be nailed in. Noggings can also be nailed between the joists where the long edges of the plasterboard will fall. The end of the plasterboard should sit halfway across the joist. This will allow the next board to butt up against it, and then, starting from the corner of the room, the initial board can be positioned. Wood supports can be used to prop up the board while the plasterboard is being fixed.

Plasterboard screws are then used to fix the board to the joists and noggings. Plasterers often prefer screws over nails because hammering has the potential to damage the joists. Fixings should be made approximately 150 mm apart. The fixings should be at least 13 mm away from board edges and 10 mm away from the factory-bound edges. Do not drive the screws in too deep because there is a possibility the plasterboard will get damaged. It is important to stop tightening once the head of the screw enters below the face of the plasterboard. A stronger ceiling can be made by staggering the boards, which helps to prevent cracks developing in the filler. Leaving approximately a 3 mm gap between plasterboards will help the filler to make firm contact.

QUESTION 1

How can joists can be found in a second-floor ceiling?

Answer:

QUESTION 2

What is another option to accurately find the joists?

Answer:

QUESTION 3

If there is no wood between joists, what can be used to add support?

Answer:

QUESTION 4

Why do plasterers prefer screws over nails when fixing plasterboard?

Answer:

QUESTION 5

Why should screws not be driven in too deep into the plasterboard and what is a good indicator to know what depth to go to?

Answer:

MATHEMATICS

Unit 4: General Mathematics

Short-answer questions

Specific instructions to students

- This unit is designed to help you to improve your general mathematical skills.
- Read the following questions and answer all of them in the spaces provided.
- You may not use a calculator.
- You need to show all working.

QUESTION 1

What unit of measurement is used to measure:

a the area of a wall?

Answer:

_____

b the amount of render required?

Answer:

_____

c the amount of adhesive required for plaster?

Answer:

_____

d the size of plasterboard?

Answer:

_____

e the horizontal length of a wall?

Answer:

_____

f the length of a chalk line?

Answer:

_____

g the cost of a renderer's hawk?

Answer:

_____

QUESTION 2

Give examples of how the following might be used in the plastering and rendering industry.

a Percentage

Answer:

_____

b Decimals

Answer:

_____

c Fractions

Answer:

_____

d Mixed numbers

Answer:

_____

e Ratios

Answer:

_____

f Angles

Answer:

_____

QUESTION 3

Convert the following units.

a   1.2 metres to cm and mm

Answer:

---

b   4 tonne to kg

Answer:

---

c   260 centimetres to mm

Answer:

---

d   1140 mL to litres

Answer:

---

e   1650 g to kilograms

Answer:

---

f   1.8 kg to grams

Answer:

---

g   3 metres to cm and mm

Answer:

---

h   4.5 L to millilitres

Answer:

QUESTION 4

Write the following in descending order.

0.4   0.04   4.1   40.0   400.00   4.0

Answer:

QUESTION 5

Write the decimal number that is between:

a   0.2 and 0.4

Answer:

---

b   1.8 and 1.9

Answer:

---

c   12.4 and 12.5

Answer:

---

d   28.3 and 28.4

Answer:

---

e   101.5 and 101.7

Answer:

QUESTION 6

Round off the following numbers to two (2) decimal places.

a   12.346

Answer:

---

b   2.251

Answer:

---

c   123.897

Answer:

---

d   688.882

Answer:

---

e   1209.741

Answer:

QUESTION 7

Estimate the following by approximation.

a 1288 × 19 =

Answer:

b 201 × 20 =

Answer:

c 497 × 12.2 =

Answer:

d 1008 × 10.3 =

Answer:

e 399 × 22 =

Answer:

f 201 − 19 =

Answer:

g 502 − 61 =

Answer:

h 1003 − 49 =

Answer:

i 10 001 − 199 =

Answer:

j 99.99 − 39.8 =

Answer:

QUESTION 8

What do the following add up to?

a $4, $4.99 and $144.95

Answer:

b 8.75, 6.9 and 12.55

Answer:

c 650 mm, 1800 mm and 2290 mm

Answer:

d 21.3 mm, 119.8 mm and 884.6 mm

Answer:

QUESTION 9

Subtract the following.

a 2338 from 7117

Answer:

b 1786 from 3112

Answer:

c 5979 from 8014

Answer:

d 11 989 from 26 221

Answer:

e 108 767 from 231 111

Answer:

QUESTION 10

Use division to solve the following.

a $2177 \div 7 =$

Answer:

b $4484 \div 4 =$

Answer:

c $63.9 \div 0.3 =$

Answer:

d $121.63 \div 1.2 =$

Answer:

e $466.88 \div 0.8$

Answer:

The following information is provided for question 11.

To solve using BODMAS, in order from left to right, solve the **B**rackets first, then **O**f, then **D**ivision, then **M**ultiplication, then **A**ddition and lastly **S**ubtraction. The following example has been done for your reference.

EXAMPLE

Solve $(4 \times 7) \times 2 + 6 - 4$.

STEP 1

Solve the Brackets first: $(4 \times 7) = 28$.

STEP 2

No Division, so next solve Multiplication: $28 \times 2 = 56$.

STEP 3

Addition is next: $56 + 6 = 62$.

STEP 4

Subtraction is the last process: $62 - 4 = 58$.

FINAL ANSWER:

58

QUESTION 11

Use BODMAS to solve the following.

a $(6 \times 9) \times 5 + 7 - 2 =$

Answer:

b $(9 \times 8) \times 4 + 6 - 1 =$

Answer:

c $3 \times (5 \times 7) + 11 - 8 =$

Answer:

d $6 + 9 - 5 \times (8 \times 3) =$

Answer:

e $9 - 7 + 6 \times 3 + (9 \times 6) =$

Answer:

f $6 + 9 \times 4 + (6 \times 7) - 21 =$

Answer:

9780170474528

Unit 5: Basic Operations

Section A: Addition

QUESTION 1

Alamy Stock Photo/William Edwards

A renderer checks the perimeter of four external wall areas that are being rendered. The lengths of the sides of the wall measure 2 m, 3 m, 2 m and 3 m. What is the total length of the perimeter?

Answer:

QUESTION 2

An outdoor wall area is being rendered. The perimeter of the wall area measures 5 m, 8 m, 9 m and 6 m. What is the total of the perimeter?

Answer:

QUESTION 3

Four truckloads of 2700 mm × 1200 mm × 10 mm paper-faced plasterboard are delivered to a worksite where a new hospital is being built. If each truckload delivers 65 sheets, how many sheets are delivered in total?

Answer:

QUESTION 4

A plasterer travels 282 km in the first week, 344 km in the second week, 489 km in the third week and 111 km in the fourth week. How many kilometres have been travelled over the four weeks?

Answer:

QUESTION 5

Over a week, a rendering company completes work on the external walls of some houses. During the week, the following square metres of wall are rendered: 32 m², 47 m², 57 m² and 59 m². How many square metres of wall have been rendered in total?

Answer:

QUESTION 6

An apprentice renderer buys a 152-mm plaster joint knife for $32, two pairs of safety glasses for $16 and two pairs of gloves for $9. How much has the apprentice spent?

Answer:

QUESTION 7

A warehouse has 20-kg bags of render stored in four different locations on site. The first location has 70 bags, the second location has 90 bags, the third location has 40 bags, and the fourth location has 100 bags. How many bags are there in total?

Answer:

QUESTION 8

A plasterer buys a 19-mm plasterer's tool for $14, a 330-mm hawk drywall plaster tool for $39, a 38-mm nail filler plaster tool for $15 and a 300 mm × 100 mm drywall trowel for $19? How much has been spent?

Answer:

_____

QUESTION 9

A client wants to use plasterboard to construct some new indoor walls. The sections of the wall areas measure 16 m² for a bedroom, 18 m² for a master bedroom, 8 m² for a laundry and 11 m² for a bathroom. How many square metres are there in total?

Answer:

_____

QUESTION 10

A construction company uses a number of 6000 mm × 1350 mm × 10 mm plasterboard sheets for different jobs. The first job uses 178 sheets, the second job uses 188 sheets and the third job uses 93 sheets. How many plasterboard sheets have been used in total?

Answer:

_____

Section B: Subtraction

Short-answer questions

Specific instructions to students

- This section is designed to help you to improve your subtraction skills for basic operations.
- Read the questions below and answer all of them in the spaces provided.
- You may not use a calculator.
- You need to show all working.

QUESTION 1

A building company has 103 20-kg bags of cornice cement stored at a warehouse. At different stages of a job, the company uses 52 bags, 12 bags, 13 bags and 11 bags. How many bags are left?

Answer:

_____

QUESTION 2

A warehouse has 500 bags of base coat in stock. If 250 bags are delivered to a worksite in one week, and a further 125 bags are delivered the following week, how many bags remain at the warehouse?

Answer:

_____

QUESTION 3

A building company uses 243 kg of pre-mixed cornice cement in the first month and 159 kg in the second month. How many more kilograms are used in the first month compared to the second month?

Answer:

_____

QUESTION 4

A floor of a new hospital totals 900 m², and has had plasterboard partially fixed to 270 m² of the internal walls. How many metres squared are left to do?

Answer:

_____

9780170474528

QUESTION 5

A short handle multi-purpose shovel normally retails for $48. The store manager offers a discount of $9. How much does the customer pay?

Answer:

QUESTION 6

A supervisor of a building company orders $5000 of personal protection equipment (PPE) for the employees. If $2756 is spent on safety boots, long pants and long-sleeved shirts, how much has been spent on the remaining safety gear?

Answer:

QUESTION 7

A building plan shows that for part of the building, internal wall areas total 96 m². Two internal walls have been fitted with plasterboard and they measure 44 m² and 17 m². How much wall area is left to be fitted?

Answer:

QUESTION 8

A renderer uses 69 20-kg bags of fine coat render over a period of time. If 105 bags were in storage to begin with, how many are left?

Answer:

QUESTION 9

The odometer of a work van has a reading of 56 089 km at the start of the year. At the end of the year it reads 71 101 km. How many kilometres have been travelled during the year?

Answer:

QUESTION 10

A company uses 31 20-kg bags of multipurpose acrylic render on one job, 29 bags on another job and 103 bags on the last job. If there were 250 bags to begin with, how many are left?

Answer:

Section C: Multiplication

QUESTION 1

A renderer charges $38 per hour. How much is earned for a 37-hour week, before tax?

Answer:

QUESTION 2

During stocktake, an apprentice counts 14 4-L containers of premix render on each pallet. How many containers would there be on 15 pallets?

Answer:

QUESTION 3

A work vehicle uses 13 litres of diesel for one trip to a worksite. How much fuel is used if the van makes the same trip each day for 18 days?

Answer:

QUESTION 4

A renderer uses 12 15-L containers of polymer high-build render on the external walls of a two-storey house. How many containers are needed for 24 houses of the same external wall area?

Answer:

QUESTION 5

An apprentice uses 33 5-kg bags of patch and prep render in a week. How many bags does she use over four weeks?

Answer:

QUESTION 6

A building company uses 16 10-L containers of texture coloured render in a week to render external walls. How many containers are needed for 12 weeks, at the same rate of use?

Answer:

QUESTION 7

A labourer's car uses nine litres of LPG every 100 km. How much LPG is used for 450 km?

Answer:

QUESTION 8

If a major building company uses 673 containers of 3-kg plasterboard finish every three months, how many containers are used over a year, at the same rate of use?

Answer:

QUESTION 9

If a labourer uses eight rolls of 90-m plasterboard joining tape every two weeks, how many are used during a year?

Answer:

QUESTION 10

A small building contractor gets a contract in the country and the workers need to travel to the worksite. If they travel at 110 km/h for five hours, how far have they travelled?

Answer:

9780170474528

Section D: Division

Short-answer questions

Specific instructions to students

- This section is designed to help you to improve your division skills for basic operations.
- Read the questions below and answer all of them in the spaces provided.
- You may not use a calculator.
- You need to show all working.

QUESTION 1

Shutterstock.com/auremar

A plasterer works a total of 24 hours over three days. How many hours are worked each day?

Answer:

QUESTION 2

A renderer earns $1400 for working a five-day week. How much is earned per day?

Answer:

QUESTION 3

To complete the plastering at four different worksites, 140 3-kg containers of wet-area base coat are needed. How many containers are used at each site if they all need the same amount of containers? Are there any containers left over?

Answer:

QUESTION 4

A supervisor's work car covers 780 km in a five-day week to inspect the work on various jobs. On average, how many kilometres per day have been travelled?

Answer:

QUESTION 5

A company requires 88 10-kg bags of cornice cement to finish some work on four separate housing worksites. How many bags are allocated evenly to each worksite?

Answer:

QUESTION 6

A building supervisor gets paid $2926 for seven days of work, including overtime for the weekend. How much does he earn per day?

Answer:

QUESTION 7

During a yearly stocktake at a major building and construction company, 2326 20-kg containers of drywall masonry adhesive are counted. If the containers are stocked in 100-container lots, how many lots are there? Are there any containers left over?

Answer:

_____

QUESTION 8

A building company orders 408 containers of 5.5-kg acrylic stud adhesive. If the containers are put into six-container lots at the warehouse, how many lots are there?

Answer:

_____

QUESTION 9

Twelve different worksites need to have 96 3-kg bags of plaster of Paris distributed evenly. How many bags are distributed to each worksite?

Answer:

_____

QUESTION 10

A building supervisor travels 2290 km in 28 days, inspecting worksites. On average, how many kilometres are travelled each day?

Answer:

_____

iStock.com/aydinmutlu

9780170474528

Unit 6: Decimals

Section A: Addition

QUESTION 1

A plasterer purchases eight sheets of 1200 mm $\times$ 900 mm $\times$ 10 mm plasterboard for $139.12, a four pack of sanding mesh for $4.34 and a 600 mm $\times$ 600 mm manhole frame kit for $19.90. What is the total cost?

Answer:

QUESTION 2

A contract plasterer buys a 220 mm $\times$ 80 mm hand sander tool for $5.95, a 280-mm plasterer's trowel for $5.55, an inside corner tool for $33.25 and an 8-mm notched trowel for $11.95. How much money is spent?

Answer:

QUESTION 3

A 6-inch plasterboard joint knife costs $31.85, a telescopic plasterboard sheet lifter costs $32.50 and a 280-mm polyurethane float costs $15.70. What is the total cost for all of the items?

Answer:

QUESTION 4

An apprentice fixes three sheets of plasterboard to an internal wall. If each sheet measures 1.25 m across, what is the total width across for all three sheets?

Answer:

QUESTION 5

Four sheets of plasterboard are fixed to ceiling. The first three sheets measure 0.90 m and the fourth has been cut to fit and measures 0.48 m. What is the total width across for all four sheets?

Answer:

QUESTION 6

A DIY specialist fixes three plasterboard sheets side-by-side to an internal wall of a house. The first sheet is 3.75 m wide, the second is 2.40 m wide and the third is 0.90 m wide. What is the width of the wall that the sheets cover?

Answer:

QUESTION 7

An apprentice renderer buys the following tools for his first rendering tool kit: a 160-mm renderer's brush for $25.00, a 280-mm renderer's float for $15.40, a rendering trowel for $16.90 and a sheepskin renderer's mitt for $21.25. What is the total cost?

Answer:

QUESTION 8

An apprentice travels 65.8 km, 36.5 km, 22.7 km and 89.9 km to a number of different worksites. How far has the apprentice travelled in total to get to the worksites?

Answer:

QUESTION 9

A plastering company is upgrading their equipment and purchases a sander and dust extractor for $2540.91, a screw gun for $475.20 and an extendable plank for $220.00. How much money has the company spent?

Answer:

QUESTION 10

Three invoices are issued for three completed rendering jobs. The first invoice is for $1450.80, the second invoice is for $1130.65 and the final invoice is for $2660.45. What is the total of all three invoices?

Answer:

Section B: Subtraction

Short-answer questions

Specific instructions to students

- This section is designed to help you to improve your subtraction skills when working with decimals.
- Read the questions below and answer all of them in the spaces provided.
- You may not use a calculator.
- You need to show all working.

QUESTION 1

The cost for 20 packets of 120-piece 150-mm orbital sanding disks is $146.40. If four $50 notes are used to pay for the purchase, how much change is given?

Answer:

QUESTION 2

A company purchases 20 5400 mm × 1200 mm × 13 mm plasterboard sheets for $1132.80. If the company's account had $8000 before the purchase, how much remains in the account after the purchase?

Answer:

QUESTION 3

A contractor completes a job and invoices the client $2789.20. The boss of the contracting company gives the client a discount of $75.50 for being one of their regular customers. What is the final cost for the job?

Answer:

QUESTION 4

An assistant renderer works 38 hours in a week and earns $729.98. Petrol costs for the week come to $48.85. How much money is left?

Answer:

QUESTION 5

A high-quality valved disposable respirator is purchased for $29.95. If a $50 note is used to make the purchase, how much change is given?

Answer:

QUESTION 6

An apprentice buys two powder-coated square notch trowels. One is a 4-mm trowel and the other is an 8-mm trowel. Both cost $11.15 each. How much change is given from $30.00?

Answer:

9780170474528

QUESTION 7

A self-employed renderer has a bank balance of $4000.95. Five boxes of 5-kg coloured render are purchased for a total of $110.50. How much money is left in the bank account?

Answer:

QUESTION 8

One side of a 2700-mm plasterboard sheet has 15.5 cm cut off to fit an internal wall. What is the width of the plasterboard after the cut, in millimetres?

Answer:

QUESTION 9

A renderer gets paid $2280.50 for a fortnight's work. If $350.90 is spent on buying new tools, $44.50 on petrol and $175.50 on food, how much money does the renderer have left?

Answer:

QUESTION 10

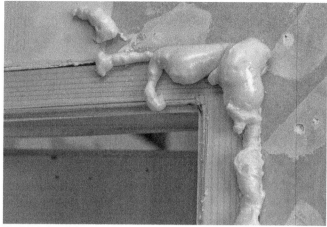

Shutterstock.com/serato

A self-employed contract plasterer has $5000 in the work account. The plasterer purchases a five-piece flush cut blade set for $35.88, three 20-packs of 320-g liquid nails for $236.73 and four 390-g cans of expanding foam for $65.20. How much money is left in the account?

Answer:

Section C: Multiplication

QUESTION 1

The price of 20-mm angle broad knives is $8.78 each. If a plasterer buys three, what is the total cost?

Answer:

QUESTION 2

A plasterer needs to purchase eight 8-mm saw blades to cut plasterboard sheets. Each saw blade costs $11.95. What is the total cost?

Answer:

QUESTION 3

One 2400 mm × 1200 mm × 10 mm plasterboard sheet costs $12.70. A company needs to purchase 40 sheets. What is the total cost?

Answer:

QUESTION 4

One 3600 mm × 1200 mm × 16 mm plasterboard sheet costs $16.65. A company needs to purchase 28 sheets. What is the total cost?

Answer:

QUESTION 5

One 2.4-m P90 metal internal angle costs $3.44.
A company needs to purchase 15. What is the total cost?

Answer:

QUESTION 6

iStock.com/kadmy

A contractor works for a building company and earns
$37.55 per hour. If 38 hours are worked in one week,
what is the gross wage (before tax)?

Answer:

QUESTION 7

A building company needs 25 10 mm × 2.4 m plaster
casing beads for work at a housing estate. Each one costs
$2.29. What is the total cost?

Answer:

QUESTION 8

A self-employed renderer needs to keep fuel receipts for
taxation purposes. His work van has a 52-litre fuel tank.
Unleaded fuel costs $1.35 per litre. How much does the
renderer have to budget for to fill the tank if there are
only two litres left in it?

Answer:

QUESTION 9

A company purchases 12 rolls of 90-m fiberglass joint
tape. Each roll costs $16.35. What is the total cost?

Answer:

QUESTION 10

An assistant renderer earns $160.65 per day. What is the
gross weekly wage (before tax) for five days of work?

Answer:

Section D: Division

QUESTION 1

A plasterer buys three 5-kg containers of 30 mm × 2.8 mm
plasterboard nails for a total of $166.50. How much does
each container cost?

Answer:

QUESTION 2

The total cost for two 120-mm paddle mixing rotary bits
is $33.40. How much does each rotary bit cost?

Answer:

QUESTION 3

A company charges $3732.70 to complete the plastering of internal walls during a renovation. If it has taken 50 hours to complete the job, what is the rate per hour, inclusive of labour and materials?

Answer:

_____

QUESTION 4

A self-employed renderer charges a client $1577.00 for working a 38-hour week. What is the hourly rate?

Answer:

_____

QUESTION 5

The cost of four 2.7-m 90° angle plastic external plaster trims is $13.16. How much does each trim cost?

Answer:

_____

QUESTION 6

An internal wall is 7 m long. If the width of the plasterboard sheets is 2400 mm, how many sheets are needed to cover the wall?

Answer:

_____

QUESTION 7

Each sheet needs six plasterboard nails to secure the sheet to an internal wall. If a box contains 500 plasterboard nails, how many sheets can be secured using the same number of nails each time? Are there any nails left over?

Answer:

_____

QUESTION 8

Shutterstock.com/rodimov

The cost of four containers of 1.5-kg plaster repair is $87.80. How much does each container cost?

Answer:

_____

QUESTION 9

A plasterer buys 24 packets of 6 g × 25 mm plasterboard bugle screws for $108.00. How much does each packet cost?

Answer:

_____

QUESTION 10

A company purchases five encasement clips for $131.15. How much does each clip cost?

Answer:

_____

Unit 7: Fractions

Section A: Addition

Short-answer questions

Specific instructions to students

- This section is designed to help you to improve your addition skills when working with fractions.
- Read the questions below and answer all of them in the spaces provided.
- You may not use a calculator.
- You need to show all working.

QUESTION 1

$\dfrac{1}{2} + \dfrac{4}{5} =$

Answer:

QUESTION 2

$2\dfrac{2}{4} + 1\dfrac{2}{3} =$

Answer:

QUESTION 3

An apprentice has $\frac{1}{3}$ of a 20-kg bag of render left over from a previous job. Exactly $\frac{1}{2}$ of another 20-kg bag of the same render has also been left over. How much render does the apprentice have, as a fraction?

Answer:

QUESTION 4

A renderer adds $\frac{2}{3}$ of a bag of render to a large bucket of water. Another $\frac{2}{3}$ from a new bag is added to the mix. How much render has been added to make the mix, as a fraction?

Answer:

QUESTION 5

An apprentice adds 1 and $\frac{2}{3}$ bags of render to a bucket of water. Another 1 and $\frac{1}{4}$ bags is added. What is the total amount of render used, as a fraction?

Answer:

Section B: Subtraction

Short-answer questions

Specific instructions to students

- This section is designed to help you to improve your subtraction skills when working with fractions.
- Read the questions below and answer all of them in the spaces provided.
- You may not use a calculator.
- You need to show all working.

QUESTION 1

$\frac{2}{3} - \frac{1}{4} =$

Answer:

QUESTION 2

$2\frac{2}{3} - 1\frac{1}{4} =$

Answer:

QUESTION 3

A plasterer has $\frac{2}{3}$ of a bag of wall and ceiling plaster patch. Half of the $\frac{2}{3}$ is used for a job. How much is left from the original $\frac{2}{3}$ in the bag, as a fraction?

Answer:

QUESTION 4

A 20-kg bag of coloured render is $\frac{3}{4}$ full. If $\frac{1}{3}$ is used on a job, how much is left, as a fraction?

Answer:

QUESTION 5

There are 2 and $\frac{1}{2}$ bags of drywall masonry adhesive on site. If 1 and $\frac{1}{3}$ bags are used for a job, how much is left, as a fraction?

Answer:

Section C: Multiplication

Short-answer questions

Specific instructions to students

- This section is designed to help you to improve your multiplication skills when working with fractions.
- Read the questions below and answer all of them in the spaces provided.
- You may not use a calculator.
- You need to show all working.

QUESTION 1

$\frac{2}{4} \times \frac{2}{3} =$

Answer:

QUESTION 2

$2\frac{2}{3} \times 1\frac{1}{2} =$

Answer:

QUESTION 3

Shutterstock.com/Dmitry Kalinovsky

There are 8 and $\frac{1}{2}$ containers of cornice cement on a pallet at a worksite, which need to be moved using a forklift. If each container weighs 20 kg, how many kilograms are there in total?

Answer:

QUESTION 4

A contractor has five half-full 20-kg containers of wet area base coat. How many containers does this make, as a fraction?

Answer:

QUESTION 5

A labourer works 37 and $\frac{1}{2}$ hours in a week and gets paid $22.50 per hour. How much is earned for the week?

Answer:

Section D: Division

Short-answer questions

Specific instructions to students

- This section is designed to help you to improve your division skills when working with fractions.
- Read the questions below and answer all of them in the spaces provided.
- You may not use a calculator.
- You need to show all working.

QUESTION 1

$\frac{2}{3} \div \frac{1}{4} =$

Answer:

QUESTION 2

$2\frac{3}{4} \div 1\frac{1}{3} =$

Answer:

QUESTION 3

A 5-kg bag of coloured render is divided into four equal parts before being mixed. How much render is in each part, as a fraction?

Answer:

QUESTION 4

An apprentice has two 5-kg containers of plaster finish that need to be separated into six equal parts for different plasterboard sheets. How much plaster finish is there in each part, as a fraction?

Answer:

QUESTION 5

An apprentice uses 20 kg of premix plaster filler for three areas, including a dining room, bedroom and kitchen. If the amount is equal for each area, how many kilograms have been used per area, as a fraction?

Answer:

Unit 8: Percentages

Section A: Adding GST to your invoices

As a small-business owner, you will be required to calculate the final total of invoices by adding 10% for GST to the total.

10% rule: move the decimal one place to the left to get 10%.

EXAMPLE

An invoice for a job comes to $2240.50 **before** GST. To calculate 10% of this total, move the decimal one place to the left. GST is $224.05.

Add this number to $2240.50. The total for the invoice is ($2240.50 + $224.05) $2464.55.

You own a business and you need to calculate client invoices to include 10% for GST. Use the above example to solve Questions 1–5.

QUESTION 1

The invoice for a job comes to $5550.90, before GST. What is the total once GST has been added?

Answer:

QUESTION 2

The invoice for a job comes to $7995.90, before GST. What is the total once GST has been added?

Answer:

QUESTION 3

The invoice for a job comes to $12 258.25, before GST. What is the total once GST has been added?

Answer:

QUESTION 4

The invoice for a job comes to $14 779.30, before GST. What is the total once GST has been added?

Answer:

QUESTION 5

The invoice for a job comes to $21 987.78, before GST. What is the total once GST has been added?

Answer:

Calculate the subtotal, GST and final total for the invoices in Questions 6–8.

QUESTION 6

Andy & Peggy's Plastering and Rendering Company	
Invoice #1	**Cost**
Reference #: 184	
Materials	$2187.50
Labour	$1986.75
Subtotal =	
GST =	
Total (incl. GST) =	

QUESTION 7

Andy & Peggy's Plastering and Rendering Company	
Invoice #2	Cost
Reference #: 185	
Materials	$3897.95
Labour	$2227.65
Subtotal =	
GST =	
Total (incl. GST) =	

QUESTION 8

Andy & Peggy's Plastering and Rendering Company	
Invoice #3	Cost
Reference #: 186	
Materials	$7886.85
Labour	$5998.50
Subtotal =	
GST =	
Total (incl. GST) =	

Section B: Saving your business money

Short-answer questions

Specific instructions to students

- In this section, you will be able to practise and improve your skills in working out percentages to help save your business money.
- Read the questions below and answer all of them in the spaces provided.
- You may not use a calculator.
- You need to show all working.

QUESTION 1

A hardware store offers 10% off the price of a small plasterer's tool that normally costs $14.00.

a What is the discount worth?

Answer:

_____

b What is the final cost after 10% is taken off?

Answer:

_____

QUESTION 2

A hardware store offers 10% off the price of a 1.2-mm T-square detach plaster tool that normally costs $22.50.

a What is the discount worth?

Answer:

_____

b What is the final cost after 10% is taken off?

Answer:

_____

QUESTION 3

The regular retail price of a dust-free hand sander vacuum plaster tool is $47.90. The store has a '10% off' sale.

a What is the discount worth?

Answer:

_____

b What is the final cost after 10% is taken off?

Answer:

_____

QUESTION 4

The price of three 160-mm renderer's brushes is $75.00. The store is offering a 20% discount in an end-of-financial-year sale.

a What is the discount worth?

Answer:

_____

b What is the final cost after 20% is taken off?

Answer:

_____

9780170474528

QUESTION 5

A render joint rake tool costs $23.00 and a 73 mm × 152 mm render edger costs $8.95. What is the final cost after the store takes off 20% for both items during an end-of-financial-year sale?

Answer:

QUESTION 6

A plasterer purchases 30 6000 mm × 1350 mm × 10 mm plasterboard sheets for $1312.50. A trade discount of 10% is given.

a   How much money has the plasterer saved?

Answer:

b   What is the final cost after 10% is taken off?

Answer:

QUESTION 7

At a '10% off' sale, a plasterer purchases 12 containers of 20-kg premix plaster filler for $38.75 each and eight containers of 15-kg joint plasterboard cement for $55.80 each.

a   What is the total cost for all the products **before** the 10% discount?

Answer:

b   What is the discount worth?

Answer:

c   What is the final cost?

Answer:

QUESTION 8

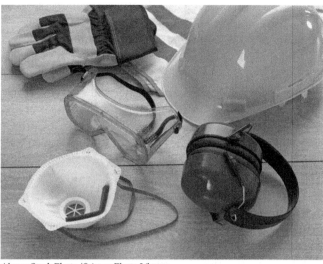

Alamy Stock Photo/Science Photo Library

A building company purchases the following personal protective equipment (PPE) at a '20% off' end-of-financial-year sale: 20 pairs of rubber safety gloves for $25.50 each, 20 deluxe hard-shell helmets for $37.95 each and 20 pairs of clear lens safety goggles for $19.99 each.

a   What is the total cost for all the products **before** the 20% discount?

Answer:

b   What is the discount worth?

Answer:

c   What is the final cost?

Answer:

QUESTION 9

A contract renderer purchases six 10-L containers of full-texture coloured render for $95.99 each, seven 4-L containers of premix render joint and patch for $35.85 each and five 500-g containers of exterior masonry filler for $13.50 each. A hardware company is having a 'closing-down sale' and is offering 30% off everything in their store.

a   What is the total price before the discount is given?

Answer:

_____

b   What is the discount worth?

Answer:

_____

c   What is the final cost?

Answer:

_____

QUESTION 10

A small rendering business has won a few work contracts and needs to buy materials for the work. The boss notices that there is a '15% off' sale at a local store. The boss orders the following materials: nine containers of 10-L medium-texture exterior paint for $135.95 each, 20 10-L containers of premix render for $68.50 each, 15 bags of 20-kg fine coat render for $31.50 each and three bags of 20-kg quick render for $19.50 each.

a   What is the total price before the discount is given?

Answer:

_____

b   What is the discount worth?

Answer:

_____

c   What is the final cost?

Answer:

_____

9780170474528

Unit 9: Measurement Conversions

Short-answer questions

Specific instructions to students

- This unit is designed to help you to improve your skills and to increase your speed in converting one measurement unit into another.
- Read the questions below and answer all of them in the spaces provided.
- You may not use a calculator.
- You need to show all working.

QUESTION 1

How many millimetres are there in 1 cm?

Answer:

_____

QUESTION 2

How many millimetres are there in 1 m?

Answer:

_____

QUESTION 3

How many centimetres are there in 1 m?

Answer:

_____

QUESTION 4

The length of a bathroom wall is 2550 mm. What is the length in metres?

Answer:

_____

QUESTION 5

The height of a bathroom wall measures 3650 mm. How many metres is this?

Answer:

_____

QUESTION 6

The length of one section of a lounge wall is 2.6 m. How many millimetres is this?

Answer:

_____

QUESTION 7

Plasterers are working on one section of an outdoor entertainment area that is 2850 mm. The other section they're working on is 3250 mm. What is the total length of the area?

Answer:

_____

QUESTION 8

Three internal walls of a house need plasterboard: the lounge room, dining room and a bedroom. The walls each measure $32.45\,m^2$, $23.15\,m^2$ and $11.85\,m^2$. What is the total wall area, in square metres?

Answer:

_____

QUESTION 9

Three separate pieces of cornice need to be cut from a length that is 3.6 m × 55 mm. The three pieces measure 1250 mm, 960 mm and 785 mm. Allowing for 2 mm per cut, how much of the original 3.6 m length of cornice remains?

Answer:

QUESTION 10

Four separate pieces of cornice need to be cut from a length that is 4.8 m × 75 mm. The four pieces measure 1175 mm, 1010 mm, 655 mm and 438 mm. Allowing for 2 mm per cut, how much of the original 4.8 m length of cornice remains?

Answer:

iStock.com/Peter Mukherjee

9780170474528

Section A: Area

> Area = length × breadth and is given in square units
> $= l \times b$

QUESTION 1

The dimensions of an internal bedroom wall are 3.5 m × 3.8 m. What is the total area?

Answer:

QUESTION 2

An internal wall of an ensuite measures 2.2 m × 3.3 m. What is the total area?

Answer:

QUESTION 3

The internal wall area for a dining room measures 3.5 m × 3.65 m. What is the total area?

Answer:

QUESTION 4

An internal wall of a toilet measures 2.1 m × 0.8 m. What is the total wall area?

Answer:

QUESTION 5

An internal bedroom wall measures 3.3 m × 3.5 m. What is the total area?

Answer:

QUESTION 6

Shutterstock.com/Bertrand Benoit

An entertainment area adjacent to a swimming pool is being rendered. The external wall is 9.5 m × 2.6 m. What is the total area?

Answer:

QUESTION 7

An external house wall that is being rendered as part of a renovation measures 3.55 m × 2.38 m. What is the total area?

Answer:

QUESTION 8

An external outdoor wall area that is being rendered measures 6.5 m × 3.5 m. What is the total area?

Answer:

QUESTION 9

An external wall adjacent to a patio area is being rendered and measures 5.5 m × 2.2 m. What is the total area?

Answer:

QUESTION 10

An external wall next to an outdoor entertainment area measures 3.2 m × 8.6 m. What is the total area?

Answer:

Section B: Perimeter

Short-answer questions

Specific instructions to students

- This section is designed to help you to improve your skills and to increase your speed in measuring perimeter.
- Read the questions below and answer all of them in the spaces provided.
- You may not use a calculator.
- You need to show all working.

> Perimeter is the length of all sides added together.
> **Perimeter = length + breadth + length + breadth**
> The unit of measurement is either in metres, centimetres or millimetres.

QUESTION 1

Calculate the perimeter of an outdoor wall area that is 13 m long × 9 m high.

Answer:

QUESTION 2

Work out the perimeter of a bedroom wall that is 3.2 m × 2.6 m, which needs plasterboard.

Answer:

QUESTION 3

What is the perimeter of an exterior wall that is 4.8 m × 3.8 m, which is being rendered?

Answer:

QUESTION 4

Calculate the perimeter of the front of a house that is 6.5 m × 2.7 m.

Answer:

QUESTION 5

What is the perimeter around a front bedroom window that measures 6.4 m × 7.7 m?

Answer:

9780170474528

QUESTION 6

Work out the perimeter of a section of a building that is 12.85 m wide × 6.35 m long, which is being rendered.

Answer:

QUESTION 7

A wall adjacent to a pool is 4.65 m × 3.85 m. What is the perimeter of the wall?

Answer:

QUESTION 8

iStock.com/aydinmutlu

A dining room wall needs plasterboard and has the dimensions of 3.75 m × 3.95 m. What is the perimeter?

Answer:

QUESTION 9

On a building plan, a patio area measures 15.55 m × 4.65 m. What is the perimeter?

Answer:

QUESTION 10

Three walls surround a pool. The measurements for the side walls are 11.75 m × 1.95 m and the measurement for the end wall is 8.55 m × 1.95 m. What is the total perimeter?

Answer:

Short-answer questions

Specific instructions to students

- This unit is designed to help you to gain an understanding about the importance of balancing the figures in your books.
- Read questions below and answer all of them in the spaces provided.
- You may not use a calculator.
- You need to show all working.

> All businesses need to balance the figures in their books to know at any time what financial position their company is in. The following ledger sheets need to be balanced and the final total calculated to account for the withdrawals and deposits.

For Questions 1−5, write your answers in the 'Balance' column to align with each withdrawal or deposit. Write the total in the bottom right corner.

QUESTION 1

Find the new balance as each withdrawal and deposit occurs. What is the final balance at the end of the week for the Let's Make it Stick rendering company?

Payee	Date	Description	Withdrawal	Deposit	Extras	Balance
						$17098.65
Chris W	4/2	Materials	$546.50			
Marty M	6/2	Invoice		$5674.50		
Kev K	6/2	Invoice		$2290.80		
Brian E	9/2	Invoice		$1668.90		
Andy H	11/2	Materials	$2285.65			
					TOTAL =	

Alamy Stock Photo/Wavebreak Media ltd

QUESTION 2

Find the new balance as each withdrawal (including 'extras') and deposit occurs. What is the final balance at the end of the week for the Revolutionary Rendering company?

Payee	Date	Description	Withdrawal	Deposit	Extras	Balance
						$22 765.40
Justin S	1/5	Invoice		$3367.75		
Jamie S	2/5	Hire equipment	$660.60			
Jeff S	2/5	Materials	$4110.65			
Jeff S	3/5	Hire equipment	$365.90			
Jeff S	3/5	Invoice		$7115.90		
Jason S	4/5	Materials	$880.25			
Jeremy S	4/5	Invoice		$3550.50		
Josh S	4/5	Materials	$12.95			
Josh S	4/5	Materials	$22.98			
Josh S	4/5	Meal			$18.50	
Justin S	5/5	Materials	$55.99			
Justin S	8/5	Invoice		$885.30		
					TOTAL =	

QUESTION 3

Find the new balance as each withdrawal (including 'extras') and deposit occurs. What is the final balance at the end of the fortnight for the Spencer & Son Plastering company?

Payee	Date	Description	Withdrawal	Deposit	Extras	Balance
						$54 772.50
Neville	1/10	Hire equipment	$225.00			
Steven	2/10	Hire equipment	$442.75			
Paul	2/10	Dinner with clients			$88.85	
Andrew	2/10	Materials	$35.95			
Neville	3/10	Invoice		$500.00		
Steven	4/10	Materials	$44.65			
Paul	5/10	Dinner with clients			$188.65	
Neville	7/10	Materials	$103.60			
Neville	11/10	Materials	$13.35			
Neville	13/10	Materials	$8.95			
Steven	13/10	Hire equipment	$85.50			
Andrew	13/10	Invoice		$1750.50		
Paul	13/10	Dinner with clients			$212.90	
Paul	14/10	Dinner with client			$155.10	
Neville	14/10	Invoice		$2990.80		
Steven	14/10	Invoice		$1885.85		
Andrew	15/10	Materials	$78.80			
					TOTAL =	

QUESTION 4

Find the new balance as each withdrawal and deposit occurs. What is the final balance at the end of the month for the P&B Rendering company?

Payee	Date	Description	Withdrawal	Deposit	Extras	Balance
						$5621.70
Bruce	1/12	Fuel	$52.75			
Bruce	1/12	Materials	$89.90			
Paul	2/12	Fuel	$65.50			
Paul	5/12	Materials	$22.90			
Bruce	8/12	Hire equipment	$225.00			
Paul	12/12	Fuel	$33.65			
Bruce	12/12	Fuel	$45.00			
Paul	15/12	Materials	$960.60			
Paul	18/12	Materials	$355.20			
Paul	22/12	Materials	$45.50			
Bruce	22/12	Materials	$760.20			
Bruce	27/12	Materials	$990.43			
Paul	28/12	Materials	$275.80			
Paul	30/12	Materials	$77.90			
Bruce	30/12	Materials	$56.10			
Paul	31/12	Invoice		$8890		
Bruce	31/2	Invoice		$7990.90		
					TOTAL =	

QUESTION 5

Find the new balance as each withdrawal and deposit occurs. What is the final balance at the end of the month for the Plaster of Paris plastering company?

Payee	Date	Description	Withdrawal	Deposit	Extras	Balance
						$2100.10
Marty	1/3	Materials	$620.65			
Rob	3/3	Materials	$1225.60			
Jimmy	6/3	Materials	$890.35			
Jase	6/3	Materials	$555.40			
Marty	6/3	Fuel	$75.50			
Rob	7/3	Fuel	$58.90			
Jimmy	9/3	Fuel	$77.83			
Marty	10/3	Materials	$22.65			
Rob	10/3	Materials	$35.90			
Marty	10/3	Invoice		$2570.00		
Marty	11/3	Materials	$1255.60			
Jimmy	13/3	Invoice		$1990.00		
Jimmy	14/3	Materials	$1170			
Rob	17/3	Invoice		$2065.00		
Rob	18/3	Materials	$1475.50			
Marty	20/3	Invoice		$2228.90		
Jimmy	24/3	Materials	$888.25			
					TOTAL =	

9780170474528

Unit 12: Squaring Numbers

Section A: Introducing square numbers

Short-answer questions

Specific instructions to students

- This section is designed to help you to improve your skills and to increase your speed in squaring numbers.
- Read the questions below and answer all of them in the spaces provided.
- You may not use a calculator.
- You need to show all working.

Any number squared is multiplied by itself.

EXAMPLE

4 squared $= 4^2 = 4 \times 4 = 16$

QUESTION 1

$6^2 =$

Answer:

QUESTION 2

$8^2 =$

Answer:

QUESTION 3

$12^2 =$

Answer:

QUESTION 4

$3^2 =$

Answer:

QUESTION 5

$7^2 =$

Answer:

QUESTION 6

$11^2 =$

Answer:

QUESTION 7

$10^2 =$

Answer:

QUESTION 8

$9^2 =$

Answer:

QUESTION 9

$2^2 =$

Answer:

QUESTION 10

$14^2 =$

Answer:

Section B: Applying square numbers to the trade

QUESTION 1

The wall of an ensuite measures 2.8 m × 2.8 m. What is the total area, in square metres?

Answer:

QUESTION 2

A wall adjacent to an outdoor area is being rendered with full-texture coloured render. The wall measures 3.5 m × 3.5 m. What is the total area, in square metres?

Answer:

QUESTION 3

The dimensions of a bedroom wall that is being renovated with plasterboard are 3.6 m × 3.6 m. What is the total wall area, in square metres?

Answer:

QUESTION 4

A building that is being rendered has a total front wall area of 13.8 m × 13.8 m. What is the total wall area, in square metres?

Answer:

QUESTION 5

Three shower recess walls each measure 2.4 m × 2.4 m and are being renovated. The recess walls need to have plasterboard removed and replaced. The shower recess also joins onto a bedroom that measures 3.8 m × 3.8 m and is also being renovated and re-plasterboarded. How many square metres in total are the two areas that are being renovating?

Answer:

Unit 13: Ratio and Application

Short-answer questions

Specific instructions to students

- This unit is designed to help you to improve your skills and to increase your speed in calculating and simplifying ratios.
- Read the questions below and answer all of them in the spaces provided.
- You may not use a calculator.
- You need to show all working.
- Reduce the ratios to the simplest or lowest form.

QUESTION 1

The ratio of application of render to the square metre area of a wall is $10\,L : 20\,m^2$. How much area does five litres cover?

Answer:

QUESTION 2

The ratio of application of render to the square metre area of a wall is $10\,L : 20\,m^2$. How much area does one litre cover?

Answer:

QUESTION 3

The ratio of application of render to the square metre area of a wall is $15\,L : 30\,m^2$. How much area does five litres cover?

Answer:

QUESTION 4

The ratio of application of render to the square metre area of a wall is $15\,L : 30\,m^2$. How much area does 10 litres cover?

Answer:

QUESTION 5

A renderer measures a wall area and the total area is approximately $50\,m^2$.

a If one litre of render covers $2\,m^2$, how many litres of render is needed?

Answer:

b If a 15-L container of render costs \$82.75, what is the cost for the render needed to complete the area?

Answer:

Shutterstock.com/Dmitry Kalinovsky

Section A: The apprentice years

QUESTION 1

A first-year apprentice plasterer gets paid $12.58 per hour. If the apprentice works for 31 hours over four days, how much is earned for the working week, before tax?

Answer:

QUESTION 2

A first-year apprentice renderer gets paid $12.58 per hour. If the apprentice works for 62 hours over an eight-day fortnight, how much is earned for the fortnight, before tax?

Answer:

QUESTION 3

A first-year apprentice plasterer gets paid $12.58 per hour. If the apprentice works for 124 hours over a 16-day month, how much is earned, before tax?

Answer:

QUESTION 4

A first-year apprentice renderer gets paid $12.58 per hour. The apprentice works for 31 hours over a four-day week. If $50 is spent on petrol, $38 on food and $57 on entertainment, how much money is left over?

Answer:

QUESTION 5

A first-year apprentice plasterer gets paid $12.58 per hour. The apprentice works for 31 hours over a four-day week. If $35.50 is spent on petrol, $47.50 on food and $62.75 on entertainment, how much money is left over?

Answer:

QUESTION 6

A second-year apprentice renderer gets paid $14.61 per hour. The apprentice works for 31 hours over a four-day week. How much is earned, before tax?

Answer:

QUESTION 7

A second-year apprentice plasterer gets paid $14.61 per hour. The apprentice works for 62 hours over an eight-day fortnight. How much is earned, before tax?

Answer:

Shutterstock.com/goodluz

QUESTION 8

A second-year apprentice renderer gets paid $14.61 per hour. The apprentice works for 124 hours over a 16-day month. How much is earned, before tax?

Answer:

QUESTION 9

A second-year apprentice plasterer gets paid $14.61 per hour. The apprentice works for 31 hours over a four-day week. If $86 is spent on tools, $49 on PPE gear and $18 on medical insurance, how much money is left?

Answer:

QUESTION 10

A second-year apprentice renderer gets paid $14.61 per hour. The apprentice works for 62 hours over an eight-day fortnight. Her fortnightly expenses include: $45.50 for clothes, $42.90 for food and $180.50 for car registration. How much money is left after all the expenses?

Answer:

Section B: Earning wages

Short-answer questions

Specific instructions to students

- This section is designed to help you to improve your Maths skills in the plastering and rendering trades.
- Read the questions below and answer all of them in the spaces provided.
- You may not use a calculator.
- You need to show all working.

QUESTION 1

A renderer works seven and a half hours per day. The hourly rate charged is $39.31 per hour. How much is earned for the day, before tax?

Answer:

QUESTION 2

A plasterer works seven and a half hours per day for five days. The hourly rate charged is $22.50. How much is earned for the week, before tax?

Answer:

QUESTION 3

A renderer works a 36-hour week with an hourly rate of $39.31. He also works four hours on Saturday and charges double the rate. How much is earned overall, before tax?

Answer:

QUESTION 4

A plasterer charges an hourly rate of $35.50. He works for 36 hours over a week. How much is earned per fortnight, before tax?

Answer:

QUESTION 5

A renderer is paid monthly and works a total of 144 hours for the month. Her hourly rate is $32.50. How much is earned for the month, before tax?

Answer:

QUESTION 6

A contractor gets paid monthly and works a total of 144 hours for the month. His hourly rate is $44.50.

a   What is his gross wage for the month?

Answer:

b   What is his gross yearly wage?

Answer:

QUESTION 7

Three contract plasterers work for a building and construction company and each works a total of 72 hours over a fortnight at a rate of $31.50 per hour each. What is the total wage the company needs to pay, for all three, before tax?

Answer:

QUESTION 8

iStock.com/Mories602

A renderer works 144 hours over a month at an hourly rate of $35.50. The renderer also works 10 hours of overtime at double the hourly rate. How much is earned for the month, before tax?

Answer:

QUESTION 9

A plasterer works 144 hours over a 20-day month at an hourly rate of $36.75. If a travel allowance rate of $39.30 per day is also paid for the 20 days, how much is earned for the month, before tax?

Answer:

QUESTION 10

A renderer works 72 hours over a 10-day fortnight at an hourly rate of $36.50. An allowance rate of $39.30 per day is also paid for the 10 days. In addition, the renderer works two Saturdays for six hours each at double time. How much is earned for the fortnight, before tax?

Answer:

9780170474528

Section C: Interpreting tables — Part I (availability and purchasing)

The table below relates to the sizes in which certain plasterboard products are available.

Thickness (mm)	Width (mm)	Length (mm)									
		900	2400	2700	2740	3000	3600	4200	4800	5400	6000
10	1200		•	•		•	•	•	•		•
10	1350					•	•		•		•
13	900				•						
13	1200		•	•		•	•	•	•		•
13	1350					•	•		•		

Use the information in the above table to answer the following questions.

QUESTION 1

a Is plasterboard measuring 1350 mm × 6000 mm × 10 mm available for purchase?

Answer:

_____

b If the cost per sheet is $43.75, what is the total cost for 12 sheets?

Answer:

_____

QUESTION 2

Is plasterboard measuring 1200 mm × 2740 mm × 10 mm available for purchase?

Answer:

_____

QUESTION 3

a Is plasterboard measuring 1200 mm × 2700 mm × 10 mm available for purchase?

Answer:

_____

b If the cost per sheet is $18.95, what is the total cost for 35 sheets?

Answer:

_____

QUESTION 4

a Is plasterboard measuring 1200 mm × 3000 mm × 10 mm, which would cover 3.6 m^2, available for purchase?

Answer:

_____

b If the cost per sheet is $22.95, what is the total cost for 27 sheets?

Answer:

QUESTION 5

Is plasterboard measuring 1350 mm × 4200 mm × 13 mm available for purchase?

Answer:

Section D: Interpreting tables — Part II (full-fastener fixing)

Short-answer questions

Specific instructions to students

- This section is designed to help you to improve your Maths skills in the plastering and rendering trades.
- Read the questions below and answer all of them in the spaces provided.
- You may not use a calculator.
- You need to show all working.

The table below provides information about the minimum number of fixing points per framing member.

Application	Board width (mm)	Number of fixing points – screws	Number of fixing points – nails
Walls	900	4	5
	1200	4	6
	1350	5	7
Ceilings	900	4	6
	1200	5	7
	1350	6	8

Use the information in the above table to answer the following questions.

QUESTION 1

If you want to fix plasterboard to a ceiling that has a board width of 1200 mm, what number of fixing points per framing member do you need if you are using nails?

Answer:

QUESTION 2

If you want to fix plasterboard to a wall that has a board width of 1350 mm, what number of fixing points per framing member do you need if you are using screws?

Answer:

QUESTION 3

A plasterer uses 900 mm sheets of plasterboard for a small bedroom and uses nails to fix the sheets to the wall. How many fixing points per framing member are needed?

Answer:

_____

QUESTION 4

A plasterer uses 1200 mm sheets of plasterboard for a lounge room and uses nails to fix the sheets to the ceiling. How many fixing points per framing member are needed?

Answer:

_____

QUESTION 5

A plasterer uses 1350 mm sheets of plasterboard for a master bedroom and uses nails to fix the sheets to the wall and the ceiling. How many fixing points per framing member are needed for each sheet for the walls and ceiling?

Answer:

_____

Section E: Scaffolding − height restrictions and hiring costs

Short-answer questions

Specific instructions to students

- This section is designed to help you to improve your Maths skills in the plastering and rendering trades.
- Read the questions below and answer all of them in the spaces provided.
- You may not use a calculator.
- You need to show all working.

QUESTION 1

A screw jack is set at a height of 100 mm and then raised to a new height of 455 mm. How much has it been raised?

Answer:

_____

QUESTION 2

Maximum platform height	4.0 m free-standing, 9.0 m with outriggers or truss base frame
Maximum working height	5.8 m free-standing, 10.8 m with outriggers or truss base frame

a The height of a free-standing frame is 180 cm. How much further can the frame be raised until it reaches the maximum platform height?

Answer:

_____

b The height of a free-standing frame is 120 cm. How much further can the frame be raised until it reaches the maximum working height?

Answer:

_____

QUESTION 3

Read the tables below, which relate to safety standards for lightweight mobile scaffold use, then answer the questions that follow.

Safe working load	No more than 225 kg
Required scaffold width	1.37 m
Required scaffold length	1.8 m, 2.4 m, 3.0 m

Type of frame	Height restriction
Base frame (with castors)	2.0 m to 2.2 m
Standard extension frame	1.6 m (4 rungs)
Guard rail frame	1.1 m

a What is the height restriction for a guard rail frame?

Answer:

b What is the required scaffold width for safe working?

Answer:

QUESTION 4

A small plastering business hires a mobile scaffold for seven days. The hiring cost is $52.50 per day, including GST. The hire company also charges a delivery and pick-up fee of $60 each way. What is the total hiring cost for the business?

Answer:

QUESTION 5

A rendering business hires a mobile scaffold for a 30-day month. The hiring cost is $49.50 per day, including GST. The hire company also charges a delivery and pick-up fee of $58 each way. What is the total hiring cost be for the business?

Answer:

Shutterstock.com/goodluz

9780170474528

Plastering and Rendering
Practice Written Exam for the Plastering and Rendering Trades

Reading time: 10 minutes

Writing time: 1 hour 30 minutes

Section A: Literacy

Section B: General Mathematics

Section C: Trade Mathematics

QUESTION and ANSWER BOOK

Section	Topic	Number of questions	Marks
A	Literacy	7	22
B	General Mathematics	11	26
C	Trade Mathematics	45	52
		Total 63	Total 100

The sections may be completed in the order of your choice.

NO CALCULATORS are to be used during the exam.

Spelling

Read the passage below and then underline the 20 spelling errors.

10 marks

Plastar and render are mortar coatings used to cover brick and blockwork. The coatings on internal walls are referred to as plaster, while the coatings on exturnal walls are refered to as render. The diference between plaster and render is the uniformaty of the mortar. Render usualy contains more cement than plaster. This is because it needs to be resistent to wether. When rendering exturnal walls, the sides of the building that receive the harshest weather need to be covered with a heaviar mix.

The most important purpose of plaster is to make the inside walls appere smooth, and to have a clean appearence that is easy to decarate if needed. Plaster or render can consist of cement, sand and water, and lime is offen added to the bach or mix. Coarse sands are considared to be the best to use for render. However, coarse sand can make the morter more chalenging to work with. Well-graded sand should be used for plaster, while less corse sand is prefferred for render.

Fix the spelling errors by writing them out with the correct spelling below.

_____

_____

_____

_____

Alphabetising

Put the following words into alphabetical order.

Plasterboard	Jointing knife
Jointing tape	Trowel
Cornice	Sheet lifter
Float	Hawk
Plaster of Paris	Nogging
Patch filler	Casing bead
Adhesive	Notched trowel

_____

_____

_____

_____

_____

_____

_____

_____

_____

_____

_____

_____

_____

Comprehension

Short-answer questions

Specific instructions to students

- Read the following passage and answer the questions using full sentences.

If the amount of cement in the render mix is increased, the workability of the render is decreased. Mixes containing less cement are generally weaker and should not be used as a primer or undercoat. In some cases, weaker mixes may be useful for application to non-rigid backgrounds. If a trowelled finished coat is preferred, a mix containing lime and cement is not appropriate because the shrinkage that occurs during drying has a propensity for surface crazing. In persistently damp conditions, check to make sure no wet render remains after it has set. Wet render may cause weakness and disintegration.

It is advised that three coats of render should be applied. The first coat is used to create a bond between the backing and rendering. The thickness of this coat should be no less than 3 mm. The mortar for this coat is added directly to the surface. The second coat fills any irregularities on the back of the wall. The thickness of this coat should be approximately 9 mm. Use a trowel to level the surface before applying the final coat. The final coat is applied to provide a clean, consistent appearance to the wall. Smooth finishes are desirable for internal work, although, with special techniques, a diverse range of textures can be created. Textured finishing can be obtained in two ways: either in the render itself or by application of a textured paint. A range of finishes can be made to the external render.

QUESTION 1   1 mark

What is the consequence of having too much cement in a render mix? Why do you think this is a problem?

Answer:

_____

_____

_____

_____

QUESTION 2   1 mark

Why is a mix of lime and cement not appropriate to use if a trowelled finished coat is preferred?

Answer:

_____

_____

QUESTION 3   1 mark

How many coats of render are advised?

Answer:

_____

QUESTION 4   1 mark

Describe the different coats and explain what role each coat has during the rendering process.

Answer:

_____

_____

_____

_____

_____

_____

_____

_____

QUESTION 5   1 mark

In what two ways can a textured finish be obtained?

Answer:

_____

Section B: General Mathematics

QUESTION 1   1 + 1 + 1 = 3 marks

What unit of measurement is used to measure:

a   the area for a wall for rendering?

Answer:

_____

b   the amount of render required?

Answer:

_____

c   the size of a sheet of plasterboard?

Answer:

_____

QUESTION 2   1 + 1 + 1 = 3 marks

Give examples of how the following might be used in the plastering and rendering industry.

a   Percentage

Answer:

_____

b   Decimals

Answer:

_____

c   Fractions

Answer:

_____

QUESTION 3   1 + 1 = 2 marks

Convert the following units.

a   1 kg to grams

Answer:

_____

b   1500 g to kilograms

Answer:

_____

QUESTION 4   2 marks

Write the following in descending order.

0.7   0.71   7.1   70.1   701.00   7.0

Answer:

_____

QUESTION 5   1 + 1 = 2 marks

Write the decimal number that is between:

a   0.1 and 0.2

Answer:

_____

b   1.3 and 1.4

Answer:

_____

QUESTION 6   1 + 1 = 2 marks

Round off the following numbers to two (2) decimal places.

a   5.177

Answer:

_____

b   12.655

Answer:

_____

QUESTION 7   1 + 1 = 2 marks

Estimate the following by approximation.

a 101×81

Answer:

_____

b 399×21

Answer:

_____

QUESTION 8   1 + 1 = 2 marks

What do the following add up to?

a $25, $13.50 and $165.50

Answer:

_____

b $4, $5.99 and $229.50

Answer:

_____

QUESTION 9   1 + 1 = 2 marks

Subtract the following.

a   196 from 813

Answer:

_____

b   5556 from 9223

Answer:

_____

QUESTION 10   1 + 1 = 2 marks

Use division to solve the following.

a $4824 \div 3 =$

Answer:

_____

b $84.2 \div 0.4 =$

Answer:

_____

QUESTION 11   2 + 2 = 4 marks

Use BODMAS to solve the following.

a $(3 \times 7) \times 4 + 9 - 5 =$

Answer:

_____

b $(8 \times 12) \times 2 + 8 - 4 =$

Answer:

_____

Section C: Trade Mathematics

Basic Operations

Addition

QUESTION 1   1 mark

A renderer purchases 36 20-kg containers of coloured render, 144 1200 mm × 900 mm × 10 mm plasterboards and 15 4-L containers of hardwall plaster. How many items have been purchased in total?

Answer:

QUESTION 2   1 mark

A plasterer purchases tools and equipment, which includes two floats for $25, PPE gear for $45 and a spirit level for $17. What is the total cost?

Answer:

Subtraction

QUESTION 1   1 mark

A plasterer cuts off 90 mm from a 2400 mm length of casing bead. How many millimetres remain?

Answer:

QUESTION 2   1 mark

An apprentice purchases PPE gear and the total comes to $124. The manager of the shop takes off a discount of $35 during a sale. How much does the apprentice pay?

Answer:

Multiplication

QUESTION 1   1 mark

An apprentice shifts five pallets of 5.5-kg stud adhesive. Each pallet has 36 containers on it. How many containers are on the five pallets in total?

Answer:

QUESTION 2   1 mark

A contractor uses 55 packets of 8 g × 6 mm bugle head plasterboard screws in a month. How many packets will be used if the same amount is used each month for 12 months?

Answer:

Division

QUESTION 1   1 mark

An invoice for a completed plastering job comes to $5578, which is the cost of labour and materials used to complete the work. If the work took six days to complete, what is the average cost per day?

Answer:

QUESTION 2   1 mark

At a yearly stocktake at a building company, a store-person counts 72 packets of 10 g × 100 mm zinc-plated bugle head screws. If 12 packets are packed into each box, how many boxes are there?

Answer:

Decimals

Addition

QUESTION 1   1 mark

An apprentice purchases a 280 mm soft-grip float for $12.80, three packets of 6 g × 25 mm bugle head screws for $26.50 and a 175-mm gauging trowel for $4.50. How much is charged for the purchase?

Answer:

_____

QUESTION 2   1 mark

An online store is selling 3670 mm × 150 mm × 35 mm steel nogging for $29.55 each, a 3000-mm screed for $79.90 and five 100-g containers of plaster crack filler for $36.40. What is the total cost for the items?

Answer:

_____

Subtraction

QUESTION 1   1 mark

A contractor working with a plasterer earns $418.50 for two days of work. She spends $35.95 on clothes and $25.50 on food? How much money is left?

Answer:

_____

QUESTION 2   1 mark

A supervisor of a rendering company purchases a blue steel wheelbarrow for $124.50. If it is paid for with three $50 notes, how much change is given?

Answer:

_____

Multiplication

QUESTION 1   2 marks

A contractor buys 23 2400 mm × 1350 mm × 10 mm sheets of plasterboard for $17.85 each at an end-of-financial-year sale.

a   How much does it cost for the 23 sheets?

Answer:

_____

b   How much change is given from $500.00?

Answer:

_____

QUESTION 2   2 marks

Four 3600 mm × 1200 mm × 16 mm plasterboard sheets are purchased at a cost of $59.55 each.

a   How much does it cost for the plasterboard sheets?

Answer:

_____

b   How much change is given from $300.00?

Answer:

_____

Division

QUESTION 1   1 mark

A plasterer earns $987.60 for four days of work. How much is earned per day?

Answer:

_____

QUESTION 2   1 mark

Seven 20-kg containers of premix plaster filler cost $257.53. What is the cost of each?

Answer:

_____

Fractions

QUESTION 1   1 mark

$$\frac{1}{4} + \frac{1}{2} =$$

Answer:

___

QUESTION 2   1 mark

$$\frac{4}{5} - \frac{1}{3} =$$

Answer:

___

QUESTION 3   1 mark

$$\frac{2}{3} \times \frac{1}{4} =$$

Answer:

___

QUESTION 4   1 mark

$$\frac{3}{4} \div \frac{1}{2} =$$

Answer:

___

Percentages

Adding GST to your invoices

QUESTION 1   1 mark

An invoice for a job comes to $3456.80, but 10% still needs to be added for GST. What is the final total, once GST is added?

Answer:

___

QUESTION 2   1 mark

A plasterer adds 10% to the order for plasterboard sheets to allow for breakages and wastage. If 187 2700 mm × 1200 mm × 10 mm plasterboard sheets are needed, how many more need be added to allow for breakages and wastage?

Answer:

___

Saving your business money

QUESTION 1   1 mark

A store has a '10% off' sale on all building tools. A customer purchases tools totalling $149.00. What is the final price?

Answer:

___

QUESTION 2   1 mark

Render products and tools are discounted by 20% in a store.

a   If the regular retail price of the products totals $1200.00, how much will the customer pay after the 20% discount?

Answer:

___

b   How much money has been saved?

Answer:

___

Measurement Conversions

QUESTION 1   1 mark

How many grams are in a 15-kg container of render?

Answer:

___

QUESTION 2   1 mark

How many metres are in 2400 mm?

Answer:

QUESTION 2   1 mark

What is the total wall area of a shower that measures 1.2 m × 1.1 m?

Answer:

Measurement − Area and Perimeter

Area

QUESTION 1   1 mark

The outdoor entertainment area at the back of a house is being rendered. It measures 5 m × 6 m. What is the total area?

Answer:

Perimeter

QUESTION 1   1 mark

Calculate the perimeter of a lounge room wall that is being plastered and measures 2.3 m × 3.3 m.

Answer:

QUESTION 2   1 mark

Determine the perimeter of a wall adjacent to an outdoor area that measures 5.4 m × 5.7 m?

Answer:

Balancing the Books

QUESTION 1   2 marks

Find the new balance as each withdrawal and deposit occurs. Write the final total in the bottom right corner of the table.

Payee	Date	Description	Withdrawal	Deposit	Extras	Balance
						$3365.80
Chris	4/8	Materials	$665.75			
Chris	4/8	Materials	$18.95			
Chris	8/8	Materials	$35.50			
Chris	12/8	Materials	$12.95			
Chris	13/8	Invoice		$1768.90		
					TOTAL =	

Squaring Numbers

Introducing square numbers

QUESTION 1   1 mark

What is 7^2?

Answer:

QUESTION 2   1 mark

An outside wall area being rendered measures 3.5 m × 3.5 m. What is the wall area, in square metres?

Answer:

Applying square numbers to the trade

QUESTION 1 QUESTION 1   1 mark

An exterior wall measures 6.4 m × 6.4 m. What is the total area, in square metres?

Answer:

_____

QUESTION 2   1 mark

An exterior wall opposite an outdoor entertainment area needs to be rendered and is 5.3 m × 5.3 m. What is the total wall area, in square metres?

Answer:

_____

Ratio and Application

QUESTION 1   2 marks

If the mixing ratio is 5 kg of tile adhesive to 1.25 L of water, how much tile adhesive needs to be added to 1250 mL of clean water?

Answer:

_____

QUESTION 2   2 marks

If the mixing ratio is 5 kg of tile adhesive to 1.25 L of water, how much tile adhesive needs to be added to approximately 612 mL of clean water?

Answer:

_____

Applying Maths to the Plastering and Rendering Trades

The apprentice years

QUESTION 1   1 mark

A first-year apprentice plasterer gets paid $12.58 per hour. If the apprentice works for 31 hours over four days, what is the gross pay?

Answer:

_____

QUESTION 2   1 mark

A first-year apprentice plasterer gets paid $12.58 per hour. If the apprentice works for 62 hours over an eight-day fortnight, what is the gross pay?

Answer:

_____

Earning wages

QUESTION 1   2 marks

A renderer works a 36-hour week and gets paid $39.31 per hour. How much is earned for the week, before tax?

Answer:

_____

QUESTION 2   2 marks

A plasterer works 144 hours over a month and gets paid $35.85 per hour. How much is earned for the month, before tax?

Answer:

_____

Interpreting tables − Parts I and II

Thickness (mm)	Width (mm)	900	2400	2700	2740	3000	3600	4200	4800	5400	6000
10	1200		•	•		•	•	•	•		•
10	1350					•	•		•		•
13	900				•						
13	1200		•	•		•	•	•	•		•
13	1350					•	•		•		

Use the information in the above table to answer the following questions.

QUESTION 1   1 mark

a   Is plasterboard measuring 1200 mm × 4800 mm × 10 mm available for purchase?

Answer:

_____

b   If the cost per sheet is $32.55, what is the total cost for 15 sheets?

Answer:

_____

QUESTION 2   1 mark

a   Is plasterboard measuring 1200 mm × 6000 mm × 13 mm available for purchase?

Answer:

_____

b   If the cost per sheet is $41.50, what is the total cost for eight sheets?

Answer:

_____

Scaffolding − height restrictions and hiring costs

QUESTION 1   1 mark

A plasterer hires a mobile scaffold for three days at a daily rate of $49.50, including GST. How much does it cost to hire the mobile scaffold?

Answer:

_____

QUESTION 2   1 mark

A rendering company is undertaking renovation work on a house and needs to hire a mobile scaffold for 15 working days. The rate to hire per day is $47.95, including GST. How much does it cost to hire the mobile scaffold?

Answer:

_____

Glossary

Arch   A curved structure that spans a space and supports a load. Arches can also be known as archways and are often used for doorways in buildings.

Arch plinth   The base upon which a statue, pedestal or monument sits.

Backing   The material that the first coat of rendering is applied to.

Bedding   Using wet mortar or plaster to set or fix a bead.

Blade runner   Used to safely cut through both sides of the plasterboard at the same time.

Casing beads   Square cornered metal beads that fit neatly over the plasterboards for protection at abutment.

Ceiling   The upper plaster surface of a room.

Columns   Vertical structures that are put in place to support the weight of the structure above.

Contractor   A person or a company that provides services or goods to another person or company, based on the terms of a contract.

Cornice   A plaster molding that is added as decoration above a door or window.

Damp-proofing   The process of coating the outside of a block, concrete or wood foundation wall with a special material to stop moisture getting in.

Double coat   A second coat of plaster that is applied to a wall.

External cladding   A protective layer that can be fixed to the outside of a building to prevent damage.

Finish coat   The final layer of plaster applied to a surface that may have more than one coat or layer.

Flat-backed archways   Arches with a flat rather than curved surface, which are often used for outdoor structures.

Hawk   A flat piece of wood with a handle on the underside that is used by a tradesman to carry plaster or render.

Interior lining   The covering or coating that is used for the inside of a building or other surface.

Joint tape   A tape used for strengthening the joins between sheets of plasterboard.

Masonry   Mortar bonds with materials to form a wall.

Patching   Carrying out repairs to cracks in existing plaster, using a putty-like material.

Plaster   Building material used for internal walls and ceilings.

Plasterboard   Also called drywall, plasterboard is made up of gypsum plaster housed between two thick sheets of paper.

Plaster mix   A combination of aggregate, binder and water.

Plasticity   How easily the plaster can be molded and shaped.

Quoin   The outside corner of a building.

Recessed edge   Recessed plasterboard has one square edge and one recessed edge. A recessed edge has a groove all the way down the edge.

Resurfacing   The method of applying plaster over an existing wall or other surface.

Screeds   A levelled layer of plaster or cement on which tiles or flooring can be laid.

Texture   The way a surface feels due to the characteristics of the material.

Two-coat system   When a finish coat is applied over a base coat of plaster.

Wall panels   A panel made of plaster that can be used to provide insulation or soundproofing. Sometimes wall panels are used for decoration.

Formulae and Data

Area

Area = length × breadth and is given in square units
Area = $l \times b$

Perimeter

Perimeter is the length of all sides added together
Perimeter = length + breadth + length + breadth
Perimeter = $l + b + l + b$

Times Tables

1

1 × 1	=	1
2 × 1	=	2
3 × 1	=	3
4 × 1	=	4
5 × 1	=	5
6 × 1	=	6
7 × 1	=	7
8 × 1	=	8
9 × 1	=	9
10 × 1	=	10
11 × 1	=	11
12 × 1	=	12

2

1 × 2	=	2
2 × 2	=	4
3 × 2	=	6
4 × 2	=	8
5 × 2	=	10
6 × 2	=	12
7 × 2	=	14
8 × 2	=	16
9 × 2	=	18
10 × 2	=	20
11 × 2	=	22
12 × 2	=	24

3

1 × 3	=	3
2 × 3	=	6
3 × 3	=	9
4 × 3	=	12
5 × 3	=	15
6 × 3	=	18
7 × 3	=	21
8 × 3	=	24
9 × 3	=	27
10 × 3	=	30
11 × 3	=	33
12 × 3	=	36

4

1 × 4	=	4
2 × 4	=	8
3 × 4	=	12
4 × 4	=	16
5 × 4	=	20
6 × 4	=	24
7 × 4	=	28
8 × 4	=	32
9 × 4	=	36
10 × 4	=	40
11 × 4	=	44
12 × 4	=	48

5

1 × 5	=	5
2 × 5	=	10
3 × 5	=	15
4 × 5	=	20
5 × 5	=	25
6 × 5	=	30
7 × 5	=	35
8 × 5	=	40
9 × 5	=	45
10 × 5	=	50
11 × 5	=	55
12 × 5	=	60

6

1 × 6	=	6
2 × 6	=	12
3 × 6	=	18
4 × 6	=	24
5 × 6	=	30
6 × 6	=	36
7 × 6	=	42
8 × 6	=	48
9 × 6	=	54
10 × 6	=	60
11 × 6	=	66
12 × 6	=	72

7

1 × 7	=	7
2 × 7	=	14
3 × 7	=	21
4 × 7	=	28
5 × 7	=	35
6 × 7	=	42
7 × 7	=	49
8 × 7	=	56
9 × 7	=	63
10 × 7	=	70
11 × 7	=	77
12 × 7	=	84

8

1 × 8	=	8
2 × 8	=	16
3 × 8	=	24
4 × 8	=	32
5 × 8	=	40
6 × 8	=	48
7 × 8	=	56
8 × 8	=	64
9 × 8	=	72
10 × 8	=	80
11 × 8	=	88
12 × 8	=	96

9

1 × 9	=	9
2 × 9	=	18
3 × 9	=	27
4 × 9	=	36
5 × 9	=	45
6 × 9	=	54
7 × 9	=	63
8 × 9	=	72
9 × 9	=	81
10 × 9	=	90
11 × 9	=	99
12 × 9	=	108

10

1 × 10	=	10
2 × 10	=	20
3 × 10	=	30
4 × 10	=	40
5 × 10	=	50
6 × 10	=	60
7 × 10	=	70
8 × 10	=	80
9 × 10	=	90
10 × 10	=	100
11 × 10	=	110
12 × 10	=	120

11

1 × 11	=	11
2 × 11	=	22
3 × 11	=	33
4 × 11	=	44
5 × 11	=	55
6 × 11	=	66
7 × 11	=	77
8 × 11	=	88
9 × 11	=	99
10 × 11	=	110
11 × 11	=	121
12 × 11	=	132

12

1 × 12	=	12
2 × 12	=	24
3 × 12	=	36
4 × 12	=	48
5 × 12	=	60
6 × 12	=	72
7 × 12	=	84
8 × 12	=	96
9 × 12	=	108
10 × 12	=	120
11 × 12	=	132
12 × 12	=	144

Multiplication Grid

	1	2	3	4	5	6	7	8	9	10	11	12
1	1	2	3	4	5	6	7	8	9	10	11	12
2	2	4	6	8	10	12	14	16	18	20	22	24
3	3	6	9	12	15	18	21	24	27	30	33	36
4	4	8	12	16	20	24	28	32	36	40	44	48
5	5	10	15	20	25	30	35	40	45	50	55	60
6	6	12	18	24	30	36	42	48	54	60	66	72
7	7	14	21	28	35	42	49	56	63	70	77	84
8	8	16	24	32	40	48	56	64	72	80	88	96
9	9	18	27	36	45	54	63	72	81	90	99	108
10	10	20	30	40	50	60	70	80	90	100	110	120
11	11	22	33	44	55	66	77	88	99	110	121	132
12	12	24	36	48	60	72	84	96	108	120	132	144

Notes

Notes

9780170474528

Notes

Notes

Notes

Notes